Leadership

Techniques and Methods of Proven Leadership That Will
Help You Discover the Real Leader That Lies Within You

*(Strategies that are Crucial to Achieving Success and
Raising Results)*

Kaspar Ritter

TABLE OF CONTENT

Introduction

I didn't start off at the front of the pack. You may be aware that in order to maintain their position as real Alpha Leader, one must be willing to battle for and preserve their crown. When I first started out in the world of athletics, I recall that the captain of the team was almost always the greatest player. They were always the kids that had the greatest influence or were the most popular. I realized at a young age that the most important thing was the impact I had on other people. When I was a youngster, I remember hearing the expression "perception is reality," but I never really understood what it meant.

As I became older, completed my education, and joined the workforce, it became immediately apparent to me that the Leader commanded the attention of everyone. They were the driving force behind it. They also brought in the highest revenue! Early on, I made a conscious decision to associate myself with such leaders. I started by inquiring and gathering information on the topic. I was interested in finding out how I might one day lead the Pack. Studying leadership was the recommendation that I heard most often. That was something that I did right away. I've read works by every major figure! Hill, Dr. Vincent Peale, Dr. Maxwell, Jesus Christ, and Carnage.

My efforts in school paid off! It wasn't long until I was promoted to shop manager, then district manager, then vice president, and eventually worked up the guts to launch my very own profitable online firm. It was not just the act of studying that was successful. It was necessary for me to transform that information into behaviors. I developed my own approach to becoming a leader. One factor, which I refer to as LIFE BALANCE, stands out as the primary distinction between my outlook and that of many other people.

When I was reading about and learning from the most influential people of our time, I discovered that more than eighty percent of them did not have a balanced life in all aspects of it. It's possible that their family life was difficult, or that they fell short financially; in any case, their physical fitness and overall health were likely suffering as a result. That was not something I want for myself. I set my sights on achieving success in every sphere of my life. What would it be like to have tremendous financial success yet to pass away due to poor health?

My life may be broken down into these four categories: family, physical fitness and health, spirituality, and one's financial situation. Permit me to clear up some frequent misunderstandings. There is no correlation between having financial success and being wealthy. It implies that you establish financial objectives for yourself, regardless of what those goals may be, and you achieve them. Being spiritual implies having a connection with who you really are on the inside. Religions may be different, but who you are on the inside is consistent.

You are able to GO AHEAD OF THE CROWD. Take the lead in all of the key pillars. When you are reading this book, be sure to take notes and go slowly. It would be perfect if you could only read one chapter each day. Take in all of the concepts that are presented to you. Take in any of the off-the-cuff ideas or insights that come to you as you're reading. Make a note of any and all ideas that come to you. Leaders are developed through time. You can and will LEAD THE PACK if you have a burning passion and trust in yourself; nothing is impossible when you have these two things.

A NEW WORLD the new manager or for anybody else who his book is created as a contrarian guide for who is in charge of supervising other individuals. It gives you a collection of tools that will assist you in navigating the treacherous management seas that are filled with sharks. It makes no difference what you oversee or what kinds of things you sell; the regulations always remain the same. I am here to assist you in achieving your goals.

Unfortuitously, the talents that got you to the position of

manager are not the skills that will maintain you in that position. If you want to be successful as a manager, you will need to acquire a new toolbox of abilities that will enable you to build effective strategies and comprehend people who are around you.

Understanding that tools are not the only thing necessary to achieve success in business is a crucial component of the "New Manager Mindset." Your desire to acquire a fresh way of thinking was the impetus behind your decision to look for this book. You are well aware that in order to attain significant success as a manager, you are going to want advice, processes, and fresh eyes. This book examines the philosophy of business, customers, systems, and people and growth. It also gives sample papers and exercises to assist you in integrating your newly acquired information. The book is structured into four parts, with each segment building on the preceding one. Utilize your intellect to your advantage as a leader if you want to be effective in your role. We are glad to have you join us.

Building A Trusting Culture

Every member of the team that you supervise is a one-of-a-kind person who has to be handled as such. Choose a present to buy for someone in a manner similar to the manner in which you devise individualized treatment programs for a patient. People's fingerprints are as unique as their personalities. Every single individual is one of a kind. You gear your talks toward the things that drive him or her to act. Think about using the same strategy to the individuals of your team. What are the things that drive your team?

The successful management of relationships is the foundation of effective leadership. Because of these connections, the members of your team will build confidence in the leadership that you provide. You will have a better understanding of the motivation and drive that your team has.

There is a distinction to be made between having a leadership role and having leadership responsibilities. Despite the fact that others will follow your directions because of your position, this does not constitute genuine leadership. Leadership entails the capacity to guide other people in such a way that they follow you not because they have to but because they want to. This is evident when you have influence on others who are not directly under your management. People will begin to follow you not because of the position you have but rather because of what you stand for. When people choose to follow you for their own reasons rather than the ones you give them, you have won as a leader and achieved your goal of being a successful leader.

Accessibility and dependable performance

It is essential for a leader to be approachable at all times. Your team members need to have the impression that they can talk to you. Being accessible forces one to consider their words before uttering them. When you are leading health care teams, it is particularly important to remember that words may be painful and erode the trust that you are working so tirelessly to develop. Simply making yourself available to your staff sends the message that they may discuss anything with you. This will result in the team disclosing their flaws, possible risks, and areas in which they see you as their leader having room for personal improvement.

The ability to adapt one's manner of operation and one's way of thinking is necessary for effective leadership. Just like fingerprints, no two people on the team are exactly the same. Individuals have a wide variety of views and points of view. Maintain an open mind and focus on developing a development mentality.

One of the most important components of effective leadership is honesty.

Keeping a clear and honest line of communication is essential to earning people's confidence. Mind your manners. There will be circumstances that call for you to have complete faith that you know your team well enough to understand what information is and is not suitable to convey. This may be a one-of-a-kind circumstance, thus proper precautions need to be taken. If you are trying to deceive your teammates, they will be able to tell.

One of the possibilities that is passed up the most often is the chance to exhibit your honesty by owning up to your faults. Even if every leader has the same goal, one of the requirements of the position is to be prepared to take chances and fall short. It's crucial to be able to accept both success and failure. It's important to be honest with your team, and one way to do so is to acknowledge when things don't go according to plan. Your capacity for persuasive leadership will develop in direct proportion to the degree to which you are honest and trustworthy.

Don't forget about good stewardship. Stop playing the blame game and accept responsibility for your actions instead.

The error will also provide a chance to learn how to effectively manage failure. You are able to rebuild your reputation by formulating a plan of action in reaction to the error. It is essential to avoid favoritism and be fair to all members of the team. You and the team will discover success in the failure. Fairness may be shown by making available to all individuals the same kinds of opportunities. You do retain the authority to decide which members of the team will be given certain chances. Make sure that everyone who expressed interest in the possibilities was given a shot at them. Being fair means you provide equal opportunity to everyone and don't give preference to any one person or group over another.

You will have superstars if you provide them with opportunity. Those members of the team who successfully accomplish the work advance their chances and stand out from the pack. They are the people on whom you can rely when you are in a bind, and they provide you the peace of mind that comes from knowing the work will be finished to the very best of their abilities. Recognize the effort that they have put out.

These remarkable people will, like everyone else, need your attention and direction. The more time and attention you provide to the individuals of your team, the more they will seek your leadership. Invest some of your time in the people' personal and professional growth by mentoring them. Have you had a conversation with them about the aspirations they have for their growth?

As a leader, people will look to you to be dependable and to set a positive example for others to follow. Show there on time, stay until the job is finished, and don't bail out halfway through. If you commit to carrying out an activity or a task, see it through to the end. If you don't follow up, it will hurt the trust that you have been building up with your staff. Every missed opportunity to follow up will result in money being taken out of the trust account.

Be willing to go above and beyond what is expected of you. Always go above and beyond what is required of you. You should be prepared to roll up your sleeves and get your hands dirty. You will have an understanding of the issues that your team faces as well as the successful procedures.

Possibilities Existing Despite The Absence Of Certainty

We had structured the existing organizational structure of the South Carolina site into specialized factories, rather than the functional structure that had been in place before, and the basis for this new organization was the value streams that the factories supported. Because of the new architecture, functional areas and the leaders of those areas are now able to take responsibility for the whole supply chain and link themselves with their commercial colleagues. Additionally, it provided the executives with the ability to operate in an entrepreneurial manner in order to manage the total profit and loss (P&L) performance, raise money for capital expenditures, devise and agree on marketing strategies with their commercial partners, and develop the talent that was allocated to the specialized factory or company.

In addition to the business alignment, the structure enabled the development of leaders, technical specialists, and operational personnel centered on the predetermined values and skills that were built to bring the company to the next level.

My meeting with the Aiken site director, Walt, and the senior vice president of manufacturing, Rob, was set to take place after all of this background work had already been completed, including the selection of leaders for the targeted factories via rigorous simulations and evaluations at the center.

Rob opened the meeting with a statement that was both straightforward and unexpected. He said, "The new president of global manufacturing, in partnership with Andersen Consulting [the original company was later re-branded as Accenture], has made a strategic decision to scrap the plans underway to establish Aiken, South Carolina, as the U.S. center of excellence." As we gathered in Walt's office, Rob began the meeting with this statement. In conjunction with this decision, the business will initiate the steps necessary to sell the Aiken location. It was so silent that you could have heard a pin drop.

Walt, who was getting close to the end of his career, was the one who established this site and oversaw it for the previous 20 years. Hearing these troubling details was really challenging for him. Both he and I were speechless from our shock. Rob added, "I know this drastic change in direction is a hard message on many fronts, and you both have invested significantly in the former strategy to build out this campus. But I'm sorry to say that I have no choice but to tell you that we will be moving in a completely different direction." In addition, I am aware that you have some concerns, but in order to allow you some time to consider your options, I will now go through the next stages.

Walt and I were given information on the next stages, and we were requested to sign a confidentiality agreement since this news and the selling procedure that was to follow needed to be handled properly. Additionally, we were given information on the following steps. There is no way that this decision might have an effect on the continuing activities at the location. My thoughts were racing with a multitude of questions about the future, the website, the individuals with whom I had collaborated over the course of the previous five years, and the way ahead for both my professional development and my capacity to continue providing for my family.

My mind was preoccupied with both the unique dynamic that comes with being accountable for an enterprise that employs hundreds of people and the personal effect that this would have on my family. For Rob, the question that immediately sprang to the forefront of my thoughts was, "What changed? What does it mean that all of the effort, plans, and messages that we have been providing over the previous 18 months have been completely turned around? What caused the transformation is a mystery to me."

Rob, a person whom I have a great deal of respect for, told me that he could give either the politically correct answer or the actual one, and he asked me which one I wanted to hear. I informed him that I would need both. The political one is going to be essential for our next encounters, but as for me, I was more interested in the truth.

In agreement, he then provided the following response: "Politically, the new president — in consultation with Andersen Consulting — has reevaluated the investment costs to build out Aiken, close the other sites, relocate, and recruit people... all within the context of the future growth projections of the business." The outcome of the review indicates that the plan should not be maintained in its current form. In addition, the commercial company has made the decision to concentrate its efforts in the United States on the businesses of dental care and gastrointestinal health.

I informed him that I had seen the figures, run the future estimates of the payback, and the numbers for continuing to operate in the present sites were beneficial to continue with the consolidation. I also told him that I had run the future projections of the payback. In addition, we spent one million dollars on the construction of a new facility and the creation of a new manufacturing technique for our most successful gastrointestinal (GI) product. He accepted the business case I presented as well as the establishment of a new and better procedure, but he underlined that the new choice would result in the mothballing of this recently built facility.

After that, I inquired about the organizational effect that it would have on the Aiken location. We came to the conclusion that it was in our best interest to hold on to a staff that was much greater than the amount of business that was currently being processed at the location. This was due to the fact that the planned growth would guarantee employment opportunities for the retained personnel. Because of this development, more actions would need to be made in order to ensure the site's continued economic viability and, without a doubt, to increase its appeal to potential purchasers. Rob confirmed that this was the case and he said that one of our top priorities for the next year would be to do a workforce study and determine the appropriate size of the business. My stomach dropped to my stomach.

After that, he revealed the non-political explanation, which was that the new president had completely bought into the advise provided by Andersen Consulting, which (in his view) was unfairly influenced by the advantages that Andersen would receive by modifying the strategy and embedding themselves inside our business. In a nutshell, the new strategy proved useful to the consultants in the company. We continued our discussion regarding the subsequent stages and the process in which we would participate, as well as the introduction of the project leader from the firm and the Andersen employees who were assigned to "work with us."

Walt, the director of the site, and I had a meeting later in the day to talk about the news, after Rob had already left. He didn't try to hide anything from me and said that he was becoming too old for this kind of thing and that he was going to start thinking about retiring soon. I let out a chuckle and said to him, "I'm not even close to 40 yet, so I've got to figure out what my future will hold."

He informed me, "Your future will be determined by how you can learn from and use this upcoming experience to develop yourself. It will all depend on how you handle it." It's not what you had planned for, but with every change comes the possibility of something better. After that, we all took some time to talk about how the news made us feel badly, simply to get it out of our systems and onto the table, at least initially.

During the Christmas holiday, as I pondered on the upcoming job that I would have to do in January, I realized that I needed to get my mind and thoughts focused on the necessity of making a choice. I also had to get myself into a good mentality about the news since, truth be told, I have a very bad poker face and I knew that I couldn't act like nothing was happening when I knew there was a lot going on behind the scenes.

It was during these musings that the following thought occurred to me: The company is being sold, but they didn't mention who was going to acquire it! Rob informed us that they would be doing a period of due diligence and searching for potential purchasers in a manner that would protect their privacy in order to find the ideal purchaser for the company.

That's it! I have the means to acquire the company! This idea shifted my mental attention away from gloom and doom and away from the sense that I was a helpless victim of my circumstances and toward the prospect that I might take active steps to influence the result.

People, the Answer Lies in the Coffee Beans

When Tom arrived to the coffee shop at precisely eight o'clock, Ryan was already there, seated at a wooden table near the window, and he motioned for Tom to join him there. Tom saw that the baristas were really busy. Tom was able to pick up on the upbeat atmosphere of the restaurant, in addition to the sounds of coffee being ground and the scent of bacon being fried. Nearly every seat at the restaurant's tables was occupied by folks who seemed to be having a good time.

Tom, how are you this morning? Please take a seat. I can't wait to have this discussion with you.

Tom took note of the fact that Ryan had not yet placed an order for anything. Do you like drinking coffee? Tom had inquired.

Without a doubt. I had been only awaiting your arrival.

The server made their way over to the table. She was on the younger side and always in a pleasant mood. What kind of gift can I acquire for you gents? She inquired with a broad grin on her face.

Tom said that he had seen that several tables had French presses. Could you please make us two coffees using the French press?

Certainly, I'll catch up with them in a moment. Which do you prefer, a light roast or a dark roast?

The darkest roast. Many thanks for your interest, Tom gave a response.

Is it a French press? Ryan posed a few inquiries.

It's the most efficient method to brew a cup of coffee. The coffee grounds and hot water are just let to rest in the press for a few minutes without being filtered through a piece of paper. You get the full taste of the coffee when you make it using a French press since the filter doesn't remove any of the oils or the flavor. There is no filtering. Although the vast majority of people probably wouldn't notice a difference, I am quite particular about my coffee.

Regarding coffee, what do you consider to be the most essential component in the production of high-quality coffee?

I really didn't give it much consideration.

Tom referred to the beans. Everything revolves around the coffee beans.

But there is a huge variety of coffee beans, with roasts ranging from light to dark, as well as a wide range of fragrances and tastes from countries all over the globe. Because coffee is a fruit, its flavor, like the flavor of any other fruit, may vary greatly depending on the region in which it was cultivated. Consider how the flavor of the many kinds of apples varies. You have to try a lot of different kinds of coffee before you discover the one you like best.

People are similar to this in some ways as well. As humans, we all have some characteristics that are what bind us together as a species. On the other hand, there are many various kinds of individuals, and each of us excels at a particular set of activities. This could only have been done on purpose. Imagine for a moment supposing there were no engineers or artists in the world. What a different place it would be.

But just as every person has their own personal preference for coffee and must search for the perfect beans, every business has their own specific requirements for talent and must search for the perfect employees. Coffee aficionados may believe coffee beans to be intricate, yet when compared to the complexity of humanity, coffee beans are rather simple.

The capacities of every worker may be simplified by breaking them down into five attributes, which helps to simplify the complexity of human people. I often make use of the abbreviation SKERT, as I indicated while I was at the gym. Acquiring skills. Knowledge and experience are essential. A look at relationships.The talent.

The competence required to do a job is referred to as a skill. For instance, in order to compile a monthly financial report, an accountant has to be able to close out the books. Acquiring information and acquiring experience are both necessary components in the process of skill development.

Recognizing A Difficult To Follow Leader

Being in a position of authority may be a trying experience. When you are in charge of a group of individuals that come from a variety of experiences and have a wide range of talents, you are under a great deal of pressure. This often leads in poor leadership, in which members of the team are not given the support they need to become successful in their endeavors. The following describes the characteristics and behaviors of a poor leader.

Has a Proud Self-Image

Even if self-assurance is a necessary quality for effective leadership, putting too much emphasis on it may have very negative consequences. When someone has an unhealthy amount of confidence, they may begin to believe that they are completely self-sufficient and do not need the assistance of others in order to achieve their goals. When one reaches this point, ego has taken the place of confidence. The success of the team is elevated to the status of a personal prize for the leader, who begins to believe that he or she was directly responsible for the achievement. There is a possibility that this individual may claim the glory for themselves while ignoring the reality that it was a team effort.

Those in positions of authority who are preoccupied with their own egos have trouble maintaining open lines of communication with the members of their staff. After that, everything boils down to just issuing commands that have to be blindly carried out. The leader no longer considers it vital to obtain the collaboration of others, which is one of the reasons why there is no clear vision or expectations expressed.

Rather than Communicates, It Issues Commands

Leadership involves collaborating with other people to accomplish a shared objective. A poor leader takes authority of a group and issues commands rather than conversing with the other members of the group. People are more likely to experience feelings of resentment and exhaustion as a result of not understanding why certain chores need to be completed. When something like this occurs, it has the potential to have an impact on the quality of the job that is produced. People are not motivated to work; rather, they feel as if they are forced to do so.

Teams led by poor leaders are unable to come together and lose their concentration as a consequence. Because there is no unrestricted flow of information, there is a restriction placed on communication. There are inconsistencies in the procedures since the strategies are not being carried out effectively. A lack of trust exists between the members of the team and the leader of the group. Members are dissatisfied, which ultimately leads to missed deadlines or substandard output from the group.

Some individuals may believe that giving orders to other people is a good method to be a leader, but this strategy will have a detrimental influence on the performance of the team as a whole. When members of a team just see their work on tasks as something they are obligated to do, the experience of working on tasks becomes unpleasant. Members of the team have a tendency to be dissatisfied and uncommitted to the project when the leader does not interact with the team and does not provide a clear vision for the team.

The Leadership Role And Power

Leadership and power have always gone hand in hand with one another. From the beginning, we have always connected leadership with power. You just cannot conceive of effective leadership in the absence of power. Is there any theory of leadership that does not include the concept of power? It's possible that this is a rhetorical inquiry, but either way, there's no need to respond. We shall demonstrate in a subsequent section that the lack of authority is not the defining characteristic that divides so-called excellent leaders from weak leaders. It all depends on how they choose to put that authority to use.

Let's take a look at the Bible to gain a better picture of how intimately power and leadership are connected to one another. There were many different kinds of leaders active throughout the time period covered by the Old Testament, as the Bible describes them. Let's take a look at two of them right now. The first of these positions is that of High Priest. In accordance with the directives provided in the book of Exodus, let us examine an example of a High Priest. Take a look at the robe and the accessories, which are made of the finest linen, precious stones, gold, and other expensive materials. The lavishness of the High Priest's robe and the accoutrements he wore would astound all of us, as is described in Exodus chapter 28, which goes into minute detail about them. In addition to the garments themselves, the High Priests were also granted access to the very finest foodstuffs that the region had to offer (Numbers 18:8-24). They possessed the ultimate authority to bless (Num. 6:22–27), as well as other ultimate powers (Lev. 10:10–11; Deut. 17:8–13). They were the Supreme Judges (Deut. 17:9, 12). They had the privilege of being the ultimate interpreters of the Law (Deut. 33:10).

Now, let's take a look at the second kind of leader that is discussed in the Old

Testament: the King. Solomon's name is the first one that springs to mind whenever we contemplate the splendor that the kings of Israel brought to their kingdoms. The monarchs had the most lavish and lavishing possessions of any other group in society, including the trappings that surrounded them. The construction of Solomon's palace took twice as long as the construction of the temple. Both his money and his renown were unbelievable. His courts went through unbelievable quantities of food on a daily basis. He also kept a large fleet of commercial ships (1 Kings 9:26-28) and was in possession of thousands of horses (1 Kings 4:22-28). The ships used to return every third year with gold, silver, and ivory as well as monkeys and apes, according to the interesting facts that have been gathered about them. (The Book of Kings 10:22) His personal symbols of royalty included royal robes (1 Kings 22:10, 30; 1 Chron. 15:27), a scepter (Gen. 49:10), an ornate throne (1Kings 10:18-20), a crown (2 Sam. 1:10, 2Kings 11:12), unparalleled wealth (1

Kings 10:14-29, 2 Chron. 32:27-30), a personal army of troops (2 Sam. According to the Bible, there was not a single piece of silver in King Solomon's palace since, during Solomon's day, silver was considered to be "nothing" (1 Kings 10:21). Keep in mind that he had 700 wives in addition to his 300 concubines. Someone said that it must have been a difficult task for Solomon to keep track of all of the anniversaries. Only the Kings of Israel are discussed in this article. If we study history, we can see that the richness, luxury, and pomp of bigger kingdoms like the Assyrian, Babylonian, Persian, Hellenistic, and Roman empires significantly surpassed that of Solomon and other Kings of Israel throughout that time period. In a nutshell, the power, riches, and height of a nation's monarch were all representations of that nation's authority.

Now we will discuss contemporary forms of leadership, including those in business, politics, society, culture, sports, and religion. What do we see, with a few notable exceptions to the rule? The power and wealth of the leader, as well as the size of their following and sphere of influence, are only some of the factors that go into determining the status of the organization that they direct. This is true even of the leaders of Christian organizations. Business in the present era teaches that strong leadership is advancing one's own interests, regardless of the price. The world of business has had a significant impact on many of the practices that are used in churches today. Instead of bringing the Church and the teachings of Christ into the business world, we have imported the rules of business and the myths of leadership into the church. The efficacy of a person may be measured by their goals and ambitions. We hold self-actualization in high esteem as a virtue, and we judge the success of a leader by the number of their congregation, often known as their "followership."

The course of human history demonstrates that authority has more often been abused than it has been used for the benefit of others. A desire to alter the manner in which powerful people use their authority has existed from the beginning of time. Will adherents maintain their acceptance of the 'Power Elite' notion, in which power is held by a relatively small number of people? Every gut feeling we have tells us that people would search for power that is "with them" rather than power that is "over them." The demand will be for "socialised power," which refers to power that is utilized for the good of society, as opposed to "individualized power," in which power is used for one's own self-interest. Employees in large corporations will eventually begin to prioritize serving a greater purpose in addition to maximizing profits. The abuse of authority with the intention of making a profit at whatever price will not be tolerated by followers. Both the yearning for righteousness and the resistance to greed will become stronger in the future. This seems to be the pattern that businesses are following for the new standard.

So, what are you going to do about us Christians? The good news is that the Bible has previously cautioned us against abusing our position of authority in inappropriate ways. Let's take a look at the God's Leadership Sketch to see how this all fits together.

Procedures For Selecting Employees

A corporation might suffer significant losses as a result of poor hiring decisions involving its employees. One employee who does not contribute as much as they should may make a project that a whole team has worked on appear awful and discourage them from continuing to work with the same level of commitment and devotion. All it takes is one person who is not in the loop to throw off the equilibrium of a team, and all it takes is one employee who does not give as much as they should to do so.

Because of this, the phase in which you recruit new employees is quite important if you want to avoid making investments in resources who have low abilities or are simply unsuitable for your organization.

In order to avoid having to pay a heavy price for this mistake in the years to come, make sure that you take the appropriate amount of time to conduct interviews and that you do not rush through the process.

There are a lot of individuals who act as if they are experts in the hiring process, including a lot of managers and HR departments. Many managers and HR departments comprehend people on the spot by having a simple conversation with them. However, things are not at all what they seem to be since you require preparation, expertise, and a strategy. In a single term, this is known as professional conduct.

First things first, do a thorough review of the available CVs, and restrict the individuals you ask for an interview to those whose profiles are engaging and are consistent with the professional figure you need.

In order to have more options, it is important to find a sufficient number of potential candidates. The first meeting may also only be conducted by the Human Resources Department of the firm, which will carry out the first screening before the meeting takes place.

It is possible that organizing the interview in various phases would be helpful:

1) Extend a warm welcome to the candidate and introduce the other participants; 2) ask the applicant to introduce him or herself, for instance by reviewing his or her curriculum vitae;

3) Inquire of the applicant on his or her familiarity with the operations of the firm and the factors that led him or her to consent to take part in the selection process; A prospective employee who shows up for a job interview without first learning about the company's primary line of work demonstrates a lack of enthusiasm in being hired for the position;

4) Describe the open position within the company, the role that the candidate would eventually cover, the type of job classification, and the expected compensation: frequently, we have a tendency to avoid talking about job classifications and compensation in job interviews (especially with younger people), leaving this aspect to the final stage of the selection process as if it were a formality. However, since you are offering a job, it is appropriate that you keep your cards close to your chest. In the event that the applicant is chosen for the position, they are needed to be informed right away of the level of commitment that will be expected of them as well as their remuneration in order to have all of the information necessary to make an informed decision about whether or not to take the position.

5) Consider if it would be beneficial to continue the conversation in a different language for a few minutes: If the expert you are searching for has to be fluent in

a certain language, you may want to attempt having a conversation in that language on a specific issue so that you can quickly comprehend the amount of knowledge it possesses;

6) You should provide the applicant with the option to ask questions; the number of questions asked may tell you a lot about the prospect's personality. At this stage, a lack of interest in the kind and manner of work may be indicated by an excessive interest in money factors (such as meal vouchers, overtime, or other business incentives) or job aspects (working hours, vacations...).

In general, you should make an effort to persuade the applicant to say as much as is humanly feasible. It is not the other way around; rather, it is up to you to decide whether or not to hire this individual, and it is up to that individual to persuade you that doing so would be the best decision.

I have both participated as a candidate and as a recruiter in interviews in which only the personnel of the firm talked, as if to persuade the different aspiring workers of how wonderful and exciting it was to work for that company. These interviews were conducted with the intention of convincing the many aspiring workers of how nice and exciting it was to work for that company.

Instead, you should focus on trying to understand people's motives for acquiring that position and how much they really care about working for your firm. This is the most crucial thing you can do.

How To Always Say Exactly What You Mean In Every Situation

When I was younger, I attended the same church with a person who had a mental disability.

This young lady went to the same high school as I did. Because she was unable to drive, she contacted me to see if I could get her to her destination.

I responded with a "Sure."

Soon enough, she grew to anticipate that after one or two instances of this, it would be OK for her to ask me to do it on a daily basis.

What you had in mind is not what I had in mind at all.

The issue was that I let my feelings of guilt to supersede my desire to be honest with her. She was in a difficult position since she had few friends who could assist her. Without a doubt, detouring to her house added twenty minutes to my travel time. Because of this, I had to set aside an hour to complete a journey that, if I had driven straight to my school from my home, would have taken me just fifteen to twenty minutes.

After two or three weeks of this, I reached a point when the torment and cost of continuing to be kind won out over my guilt. When I left her off at her home for the final time, I made the decision to face her there.

"Julie," I said to her, "I'm sorry, but I'm not going to be able to pick you up for school any more."

I sat back and waited for her to completely unravel.

She had a look of resignation as she answered, "Okay," and then got out of the vehicle.

Taking Layers Off of the Onion

As my unease increased, I came to the conclusion that she was using me for her own benefit by taking advantage of me. She was aware of my reputation as a kind and submissive person who never stood up to anybody. As a result, she had the following thought: "Hey, maybe I can get some free rides to school and not have to ride that smelly city bus."

And since she had a disability, I believed her story without question.

You have to realize that she was using my sense of guilt as a tool to manipulate me.

It wasn't until my uneasiness reached the point where it couldn't be ignored that I worked up the nerve to approach her about it.

How much time and energy would I have saved, not to mention how much pain, if I had uncovered her objectives and conveyed my expectations from the very beginning?

There Are Times When Communication Breaks Down Well

A significant portion of the suffering in our life is brought on by the fact that we do not express our true feelings. We don't say what we really want to say because we're frightened of upsetting someone else's sentiments. However, when we act in this manner, we bring about the conditions necessary for us to eventually do harm to another person. When that time comes, the wound won't be only superficial.

Another thing that concerns us is the idea that the other person, after hearing what we desire, may draw her sword and attempt to murder us after we've told them what we want. However, there is a good probability that won't be the outcome. It's possible that she'll merely agree with you by nodding her head and saying "Okay."

When a butcher knife suddenly flies behind you, it's an unusual occurrence that requires you to guard your back.

How to Communicate Exactly What You Mean

If you communicate properly, you will not only help yourself, but also your coworkers, save a lot of time and save a lot of hassle. Here are three things you may do to work toward achieving that goal.

1. Keep it Straightforward and Uncomplicated.

All too often, we water down what we have to say in order to make it seem less harsh. However, if we do so, we run the risk of completely neutering the effectiveness of our message. Keep it straightforward by using concise statements like "I need your help."

"Are you going to find someone for me?" "Will you get someone for me?"

"Would you be able to take me to school on Thursday morning?"

These assertions are clear, uncomplicated, and go right to the point. The majority of the questions may be answered with a yes or no, and those answers can be followed up with more specifics.

Keep in mind that working your way around a shrub will never result in its removal.

2. Be Willing to Commit an Offense for the Right Reasons.

Only the most brazen individuals would intentionally cause offense just for the purpose of doing so.

Being in close proximity to someone like that may be rather irritating. I recommend that you tell them how bothersome they are in a manner that is simple and straightforward.

There is always the possibility that what you say may be taken the wrong way by another person. Keeping this in mind, make sure that you always allow the appropriate response determine what you say to someone. At least in this sense, they have been insulted for the reasons that should be considered offensive. Put yourself in their shoes and ask yourself, "Will saying this be for the greater good of the group?" Will she become a better person as a result of it? Will it assist her in becoming a more efficient worker? If you have the ability to respond with a "Yes," then you should go ahead and say it.

A word of caution, however. Maintain a straightforward and easygoing tone. Avoid making it a personal attack. Please refrain from calling her an idiot. Bring attention to the fact that her activities may not be prudent. And then explain to her how she should steer clear of such situations in the future.

3. You Should Never Hold Grudges If You're in the Wrong.

You are, after all, just human. There will be instances when you mess up. Be humble enough to recognize your mistake and offer an apology. It's possible that other folks are also correct. Because you are so dedicated to doing the right thing, you won't take it personally when other people point out your errors.

And when everyone is able to do that without being overtaken by feelings of guilt, then the entire group will be able to go on.

But hear me out. There are moments when we do in fact injure one another. It is impossible to change the situation. Isn't it true that when you're weary, your emotions become more delicate and sensitive? When you're under a lot of pressure, it's easy for rage to hide in the shadows, just waiting for the proper moment to emerge. Take it into consideration. If you really must express anything that someone may find offensive, condense what you have to say as much as possible.

After all, messes that aren't as big are much simpler to clean up, don't you think?

Make Your Mark on History Through Your Words.

Effective communication is a challenge for many people. However, proceed. Take the risk of upsetting others in order to keep doing the right thing. Keep in mind that you are interacting with emotional animals that may occasionally utilize rationality. People are the ones you must deal with. When we do utilize reasoning, it is almost often to defend the choices that we have already made.

If you are able to utilize the reasoning of the other person to demonstrate why doing what is right is preferable, then you probably have a good chance of leading the whole globe.

If you put these suggestions into practice, you will eliminate a significant number of the communication issues that arise as a result of not doing so. Then, when you do run into an issue, you may turn to these strategies for assistance in overcoming it.

And if you are able to communicate what you mean on a consistent basis, the people who follow you will always have faith in you. Why? Because there won't be any pleasant surprises in store for me. They will be aware that you will tell them the truth at all times. They will see you as someone who can find solutions to problems.

Discover More About The People That Follow You.

You are free to start concentrating on your followers now that you have an understanding of the environment in which you will exercise your leadership. In general, you are interested in learning about the most effective approach to put your human resources to use in order to achieve the objectives of the business.

that are the people that follow you?

Do you make your own contributions individually?

To get started, you need to determine the different categories of individuals that you will be guiding. Every person in the company begins their time there as an individual contributor. Even though they are often the lowest level jobs on the organizational chart, you may begin honing your leadership abilities right away if you start working in one of these roles. At this point in the game, your objective is to lead oneself in order to enhance the individual contributions you provide to the company. Being reliable is another way you may start constructing a reputation for yourself as a leader.

Are you in charge of something?

If you have a managerial position in your organization, there is a good probability that you are in charge of a team of people that are considered individual contributors. When a corporation promotes you to a management position, they do it with the presumption that you are already an expert in your previous role as a contributor. Your mission is to educate your followers on how they may better their own personal performance using the information you have gained. You assist other people become more productive and effective in their work by drawing on the experience you've gained by being a contributor.

Do you have what it takes to lead the leaders?

You will eventually advance to a position where you are in charge of supervising other leaders. Typically, those who work in the field of human resources are hired for jobs like this one. If you do not have previous experience serving as a manager or leader of individual contributors, it is strongly recommended that you do not accept a job similar to this one.

Do you serve as a leader in the organization?

If you go further in your career, you will have the opportunity to become a leader who is responsible for making changes in the policies that apply to the whole firm. When you receive a position like this, you are immediately put in charge of running whole departments and divisions. Vice Presidents of firms often hold these positions in most businesses.

Do you hold the most senior leadership position in your organization?

Last but not least, you can potentially be entrusted with the responsibility of leading large enterprises. This sort of job often falls on the shoulders of the President or CEO of a company. When compared to leaders at lower levels, those in this position need a unique set of talents in order to succeed.

To be this sort of leader, you need to have a clear picture in your head of the kind of company you want it to evolve into. If the firm has already achieved its maximum level of productivity, this kind of leader looks for ways to reimagine the business in order to give it a new lease of life and ensure that it will continue to expand.

The duty that one must shoulder whenever they hold a position of significant influence.

Your previous achievements in leadership will have a greater impact on the company as a whole to the extent that your decision-making power will expand as you rise through the ranks of your company and assume positions of increasing responsibility. In the event that you are a manager, the decisions that you make will solely have an effect on the section of the business that you are accountable for. However, as you progress in your career and become a regional director, the decisions that you make will now have an effect on several branches within a certain region because of the scope of your new responsibilities.

As a consequence of this fact, the stakes associated with your decision-making have increased. If you are in one of these higher positions and make mistakes in decision-making, the amount of money lost and the implications linked to business will be bigger if you are in a higher position in the company.

People who occupy higher positions of leadership within an organization are the ones who are accountable for making changes that will have an impact on the firm over the longer term. These changes will have an effect on the company both immediately and in the future. The vice presidents and the chief executive officers of the corporation are responsible for making long-term reforms that place an organization in a more competitive position to compete in the future.

What Constitutes An Effective Leader?

You need to have an understanding of the characteristics of effective leaders in order to develop your own leadership skills. There is a good chance that you already have some level of proficiency in each of the talents that are mentioned here. There are going to be certain abilities that you are better at than others. These are going to be the ones. The most essential thing is to achieve a good equilibrium between all of your talents. This chapter is going to highlight some of the most significant attributes that a successful leader should possess, as well as provide you with some pointers and suggestions on how you might develop the talents that you currently have.

Integrity: Good leaders treat people the way they would want to be treated themselves, just as the majority of us have been instructed to do since we were children. They have strong morals and feel that being truthful is the most important factor in achieving one's goals. Leaders that are honest provide facts to their teams in an open and transparent manner and refrain from embellishing the truth in any way. Because their leader is always honest with them, the team always tells the leader the truth about where they stand with the leader, and because the leader is always honest with the team, the team always tells the leader the truth about where they stand with their leader.

Empathy: The most effective leaders are those that publicly laud their teams and privately handle issues with their teams while demonstrating real care. Strong leaders are ready to steer their teams through difficult situations and are always on the lookout for improved solutions that will contribute to the long-term success of the group they are leading. Instead than seeking for someone to place blame on, effective leaders concentrate their efforts on finding positive solutions to problems and moving ahead. It is more probable that members of a team will go the additional mile for their leader if the team's leader demonstrates empathy for the members of the team they are leading.

Positivism Great leaders are optimistic people who exude a positive vibe that their colleagues feed off of. Optimistic leaders always seem to have a solution and know what to say to encourage and reassure their people. They always seem to have a solution. They steer clear of negative thinking and steer clear of criticizing themselves. Because these leaders are always looking at the bright side, their team members are more confident in their work and know that their leader will find a solution to any problem. These leaders are always trying to gain consensus and get people working together as a team in an effective and efficient way.

Accountability requires that leaders be prepared to accept responsibility for the performance of themselves as well as everyone else in the group. They are quick to see issues when they develop and immediately begin looking for ways to resolve them so that things can get back on track. Leaders who are accountable check in on their staff, keep an eye on how well the company's rules are working, and follow up on any problems that haven't been resolved. Because of this, the members of a team are able to have the confidence that their leader will assist them in being successful and will not give them work that is above their skills without providing them with the appropriate guidance.

Confidence: It's easy to catch someone else's confident attitude. People are naturally attracted to leaders who exude confidence; they seek their counsel and, as a result, experience an increase in their own level of self-assurance. A self-assured leader is one who is able to maintain their ideas, methods, and views even in the face of opposition because they are aware that these things are the product of extensive research and a great deal of effort. Confident leaders are prepared to accept responsibility and move fast to fix the conditions under their power when they are shown to be incorrect. People who work under a leader who exudes self-assurance are more inclined to emulate that trait themselves. These individuals are also aware that they can depend on their leader to advocate on behalf of the whole team.

Leadership requires decisiveness since difficult choices often need to be made. Leaders have a responsibility to realize that in some circumstances, tough choices must be taken in a timely way while taking into account what is in the best interests of the business as a whole. Leaders that are decisive are aware that making judgments requires a solid authority and a sense of finality. They are also aware of when it is appropriate to encourage collective decision making. Those who follow leaders who are able to make clear choices may have faith that their leader will steer them in the right direction even in the face of challenges. A leader who is decisive inspires confidence in his team, provided that the leader also understands when to stop and listen to what his team has to say.

Aware: Leaders are conscious of the fact that there is a distinction between management and employees, as well as between supervisors and their subordinates. They are aware of and comfortable with this distinction. They are able to differentiate themselves from their staff in a manner that enables them to keep an impartial perspective on everything that is happening inside the company without implying that they are in any way superior to their colleagues. This enables their followers to be aware of who is guiding them and to have faith that their leader is always going to steer them in the appropriate path so that they may accomplish the goals they have set for themselves.

Main idea: Effective leaders are able to think ahead and maintain a high level of organization. They give careful consideration to the many outcomes that might result from their selections as well as the options that are now available. When they are ready, the next step is to devise a method, a strategy, and a routine that are all directed toward their success and can be readily defined, monitored, and analyzed. They are able to convey their plans to the important participants, and they also have backup plans in place in case an additional one becomes necessary at the very last minute. Those who are following can see that their leader is someone who is committed to ensuring that they attain their goal, despite of the challenges they face along the way. This gives those who are following the confidence to go on.

When all of these qualities are present in a leader, you have a leader that actually inspires others to follow in their footsteps. A genuine leader is someone who is able to express ideas in a way that is both clear and succinct, and who inspires others on a daily basis. They motivate their team to perform at a higher level by presenting them with challenging goals that are still within reach, and they provide their team all of the support and resources that are required to accomplish those objectives. Your team is going to know and understand that you are looking out for the interests of the whole team and that you are devoted to seeing the team succeed if you have a mix of the attributes that were listed above. This is going to guarantee that you are an effective leader.

Take into consideration the questions that follow:

Which three of the aforementioned characteristics best represent you?

Which three of the aforementioned characteristics do you believe you have the greatest room for improvement in?

Are you of the opinion that a successful leader has to possess all of the qualities listed above?

In order to be a great leader, it is essential to have a healthy balance of all of the qualities listed above. If you are strong in some of the talents but not others, you are likely to discover that you fall into one of two categories: either the "generalist" category or the "specialist" category.

1. Although you are able to create and establish solid outcomes with people, you often fail to complete the things you set out to do, and you frequently struggle to encourage your team to get their job done.

2. You always have a clear vision of what you want to achieve, and you know what you need to do to make sure that your team is working on the area of the project that is most suited to their abilities. Nevertheless, you sometimes forget that the members of your team are individuals, each of whom has their

own requirements and requirements of their own.

We are going to discuss what you can do to help you improve on each of the characteristics that excellent leaders have, and this will help you boost the level of skill that you already have. Now that you are aware of the characteristics that good leaders have, we are going to discuss what you can do to help you improve on each of these characteristics. By demonstrating to yourself that you are prepared to become a greater leader than you have ever been before, all you need to do is spend some time working on enhancing each of the characteristics stated above.

The Science And Practice Of Influence

The art of persuasion is more closely related to science. The majority of people have the misconception that persuasion is a difficult trade that takes years to learn. They believe that the only individuals who ever genuinely master this talent are magicians and persons who sell secondhand vehicles.

Convincing someone of anything is much simpler than this. In its purest form, the art of persuasion consists of influencing others to agree with you by conveying to them the appropriate information in the appropriate sequence. The majority of us are familiar with the appropriate statements; the issue lies in delivering them in the appropriate sequence. That is the art and science of convincing others.

It's true that convincing someone of anything is a process, but it doesn't have to take months or even days to be successful. It's not unusual for me to make a new connection and complete a transaction inside the same hour. People send me money even though they have only known me for a little over an hour. You have already read quite a few chapters of this book, and as a result, you are aware that I am not very articulate. I'm not a skilled orator with a sweet-sounding voice. When it comes to the art of persuasion, the sequence of events is of far more significance than the words themselves.

At the beginning of the training for every sales career, you will learn about "yes ladders." First get someone to agree to something tiny, and then ask them to agree to something somewhat more significant. Never give up, because sooner or later they will agree to make the transaction. This is a straightforward progression from a little yes to a huge yes, but it serves as an excellent illustration of the point. If even one of your inquiries is out of sequence, the whole ladder will be rendered useless.

Commence the Fight... To begin,

Whoever does the most studying and preparation for a certain situation, whether it an event or an interaction, is the one who comes out on top. When you have more information at your disposal, it is much simpler to be successful and effective when you are interacting with another person.

There are primarily two kinds of research methods. There is broad research, in which you learn all there is to know about the kind of people you are going to be engaging with and all the advantages of what it is that you can provide. It is simple to build credibility when you have a good understanding of who you are; it is simple to develop competence and exhibit your knowledge when you have done the necessary study and preparation. When you understand what people at an event have in common with each other, it is much easier to build casual relationships with them.

On a further, more in-depth level, there is the practice of preparing for certain individuals. Researching a person's business model, their attitude, the way they do business, and their interests enables you to connect with them on a deeper level after you have already established a professional relationship with them. You find out that they have a strong interest in golf, adult literacy, or that they make regular donations of blood - these are the topics that people discuss in interviews broadcast on the radio, articles published in newspapers, blog posts, and podcasts. We are able to learn the specifics of individuals and so prevent ourselves from making catastrophic errors.

My acquaintance once went up to a prominent member of the business community in order to extend an invitation to attend a party that we were holding. And because of it, the connection was terminated for good.

My buddy made a critical error when they offered a generic connection to the one individual who was an exception to the rule. You may invite ninety-nine percent of people to an amazing party filled with models, drink, fun, and good times, and it will work at the events that are being discussed here. But he did manage to identify one individual who is an exception to the general norm. And it is precisely in this area when the specificity of your study has a significant impact.

If my buddy had listened and recalled that this possible ally was married with children and did not drink, he would not have brought up the subject of his upcoming wedding but rather would have spoken about his plans to be married. That would have provided him with the true middle ground to stand on.

My capacity for study has been a major contributor to my achievements, as has the fact that I begin preparations for my activities months in advance. I attend a maximum of two events each calendar year. That indicates that I need to be extremely productive in order to keep and build my company. This is the case whether I go to an event or a conference, or if I meet a celebrity or someone I want to do business with. This is a really significant window of opportunity. Because traveling to these events might either cost you a significant amount of money or a significant amount of time, you naturally want to maximize the return on your investment. You need to make sure that you receive a good return on your investment, but you can't afford to spend thousands of dollars every week traveling to several events until you find one that is successful.

The time you invest in organizing and preparing the battleground is going to pay off in a far bigger way than the time you spend conversing with other people. What comes before and after an event are the most important factors in determining its overall outcome. The more thorough your preparation is, the more you will know exactly what it is that you want, who you are going to talk to about it, and what you are going to do to get it. Because of this, you are able to develop relationships. You are able to find common ground if you are aware of the things that individuals like and the things that interest them. You have the ability to establish a genuine rapport, and as a result, you have the potential to be the only one that they remember, given that you are the only individual with whom they established a genuine connection.

You may think of this as either preparing the battlefield, in which case we would be making particular preparations for a place, or preparing to convince, in which case we would be preparing our attitude and our knowledge. Either way, the end goal is to accomplish something. These are the two concrete methods that we may prepare ourselves before going to an event, before meeting somebody, and even before beginning the process of actively persuading someone. The one who gets a head start on the preparations is the one who will end up having the greatest success overall.

Developing A Leadership Mentality And Attitude

Consider some of the people whose leadership you look up to. You routinely interact with leaders in all facets of your life, whether it be at work, in the government or sports, or in a social group; whether it be via direct interaction or by observation from a distance. You have most likely seen that some leaders enjoy greater levels of success than others. While some individuals are able to guide their teams to incredible successes, others have a far more difficult time getting their teams to do anything. Leadership is a multi-faceted issue, and there is no magic formula that, if followed, would immediately make you a better leader. However, there are some general guidelines that may help. The path to being a successful leader is paved with hard effort. Academic experts have generated a wide number of hypotheses throughout the course of time on the qualities that make someone a good leader. None of these ideas offers a conclusive response to the issue of what characteristics are necessary in an effective leader. There will be moments when you are a part of a team working under the direction of someone else, and there will be other occasions when you will be asked to lead the group. While some of the teams that you are a part of are sure to achieve great success and wow everyone with their output, others won't be able to accomplish what they set out to do. Being a part of or even the leader of a group that is successful in achieving its goals is always an amazing experience in its own right.

The Mindset Required for Leadership

My viewpoint is that everyone has the potential to step into a leadership role. In this book, I will not provide you with a detailed recipe outlining the particular procedures that need to be carried out in order for you to become a leader. The process of interacting with other people is just too intricate for that. I will provide you a set of tools that will direct you in improving the leadership talents that you currently possess, and they will be provided to you as a set. You are going to put these strategies to work in order to establish a leadership mindset. A method of thinking about the relationships between people is what we mean when we talk about having a leadership mindset. It directs the activities of the leaders as they learn what factors contribute to the success of groups of individuals working toward a common objective. Excellence in leadership is directly proportional to one's level of conceptual comprehension. You will continue to build the capabilities that will allow you to be a successful leader if you acknowledge the important characteristics that are shared by skilled leaders and make a conscious effort to cultivate those characteristics within yourself.

The Six Core Competencies Necessary for Effective Leadership

You have, throughout your life, seen leaders who consistently directed groups of people with high levels of performance. The leaders who you considered to be the most effective all had a set of qualities in common that increased the likelihood of success for both themselves and the organizations that they oversaw. The standard of leadership that you consider to be the most successful is one that is sometimes referred to as transformational leadership, which is one of the various ways that one might think about leadership. The method of transformational leadership results in constructive change. The most transformational leaders craft a mission statement that serves as a compass for their teams. They inspire and drive the people who follow them to create, change, and develop themselves. These leaders provide their teams with the inspiration necessary to accomplish important goals. They not only act as examples for the rest of the team to follow, but also foster an environment that encourages members to grow into capable leaders. The following is a list of features and attributes that are shown by outstanding examples of transformational leadership. In the next chapters, we will go more thoroughly into each of these traits, and you will discover what you can do to enhance the leadership abilities that you currently possess. In addition, we will discuss some other characteristics that are associated with effective leaders.

Control Of One's Feelings

There is a good chance that there are characteristics that a person has that you find abhorrent. The majority of these features come from their poor conduct. As a direct result of this, individuals in our day-to-day lives suffer negative emotions and attitudes. These features are mostly made easier when an individual has been harmed or when unexpected occurrences or experiences take place. Victims of these kinds of events are more likely to display negative feelings.

These feelings might be harmful to the persons to whom you are related. For instance, a woman may be subjected to the wrath and insults of her husband on a regular basis. As a consequence of the detrimental impacts they cause, these destructive habits are referred to as vices in the culture. These kinds of impacts may lead to a wide variety of illegal behaviors, including homicide, domestic violence, and many more. It is thus up to you to maintain control of the inappropriate feelings so that you do not end up on the incorrect side of an argument. If one is going to learn how to deal with them, then one must first get familiar with the reasons that are described below.

Some of the factors include ones' upbringing and the culture in which they were raised. The greatest amount of an individual's beliefs are likely to have been formed by either their parents or society as a whole. Some of the vices are even passed on from the guardians to their charges. They say that "like father, like son," therefore it stands to reason that if your role model has a negative disposition, you will most likely take like them in that regard. At other instances, an individual's identity is formed by the teachings of their society.

Negative feelings are sometimes acquired as a result of one's exposure to heinous acts and circumstances. If some people have done you wrong in the past, you will be furious with them no matter what it takes. When you emerge on the other side of a traumatic experience, you are always left with a terrible impression and a plethora of unpleasant emotions. Therefore, as a consequence of this, you are likely to blame other people for your misfortunes and to have a gloomy outlook on a certain topic.

When one compares himself to others, it makes them more irritable if they discover that another coworker is superior in some aspect. People need to realize that everyone has a unique set of skills and abilities. Therefore, do not judge your own abilities based on those of others. In this scenario, you will fail to see your own potential and will consider the accomplishments of others to be flawless. That is where poor self-esteem comes from in the first place. Consider the behaviors of people who have poor self-esteem, which often include being angry, resentful, spiteful, afraid, and hateful of others.

When you put the desires you have for yourself in front of other people, it generates a negative attitude. That is the point at which you feel the need to compete with other individuals, and you acquire an attitude of jealousy if others achieve success. You are always gluttonous in the sense that you want to have everything available to you. When other people don't treat you like you expect them to, you feel fury. You should nevertheless exhibit some pride in order for people to acknowledge your existence.

You should begin by determining the unfavorable feeling that you have inside of you. It's possible that other people have characterized you as prideful, greedy, or temperate. There are some mindsets that can only be revealed to you by your peers in certain fields. Do not be hesitant to question even your closest friends what it is about you that they cannot stand to see occasionally. You might be under the impression that everything is going swimmingly, yet some of your habits are rather nasty. Consider a period when you were the cause of some mayhem and the role you played in the conflicts that ensued. When you are aware of the poor attitude you have, you are in a better position to consider how to alter it.

You may try meditating on the influence that feeling has on you. There was probably a moment when you were completely overcome with wrath, and you physically attacked another person. Due to this reason, the connection with that individual was severed. Or you may have alienated some of your closest friends because you were too arrogant to prioritize your interests above those of your pals. When you fully comprehend the devastating effects of that habit, you will immediately begin to consider the many options available to you in order to make a difference. Always make the effort to make amends with the coworker you have mistreated and enquire about how they anticipate you will conduct the next time.

Investigate the background of that snobbish attitude or condescending personality. You cannot put up a struggle against anything if you do not understand where it came from. It is never inappropriate to take a critical look at the factors that led to the problem. It is possible that you may be astonished to learn that the cause is something that you did not anticipate. Consider the example of a guy who is haughty due to the fact that he is the best swimmer in the world. To be clear, there is nothing inherently unethical about becoming the best swimmer in the world; but, it is unethical to exaggerate the extent of your achievement. Therefore, in the circumstance, you need to keep your cool and acknowledge the difficulties you face.

One may become better equipped to cope with a certain challenge by reading about or discussing their feelings of anger with other individuals. You could believe that you are the only person in the world who suffers from a personality disorder, but in reality, many others do. Make it a point to discuss with them how they overcame the obstacles presented by their villainous personas. It can come as a surprise to learn that what you are going through is not nearly as difficult as what they are going through right now. Learn how to deal with a scenario like this by reading relevant publications or doing research on the topic online. Permit your close friends or family to provide you with feedback on your behavior. During the procedure, they will provide advice on how to most effectively deal with the feeling.

Changing unjustified attitudes may also be accomplished by working on improving one's emotions. It is not a question of how you can get rid of your discomfort; rather, it is a question of how you can enhance the negative feelings in accordance with the situation. For instance, a person can be suffering from dread and worry, yet it is possible to regulate these feelings. If you find that you are uncomfortable speaking in front of a large audience, try practicing your presentation skills in front of a more intimate audience beforehand. Engage in conversations with other people, such as friends or psychologists, who may provide you advice on how to modify your conduct.

Maintain a level of effective control over your attitude. After being familiar with your mood and its influence, the next step is to become knowledgeable about how to exercise control over it. If you have a hot temper, you have to train yourself to keep your cool no matter what the situation is. If at all feasible, plan out the various control mechanisms and put them in writing. You may even ask someone to wake you up when you experience that feeling by telling them to alert you. You will eventually be able to check yourself and attempt to manage a situation as soon as you sense the behavior coming. This will take some time. You will eventually get used to doing this, but eventually you will break the habit.

Try to find the best possible business. If you surround yourself with individuals who consistently have bad feelings, there is no possibility that you will ever change. On the other hand, you will take on their characteristics if you surround yourself with role models and emotionally sophisticated men. This undesirable mentality will soon be eliminated from our midst. By participating in these interactions with other people, one is able to determine whether or not their actions are acceptable. If they are pleased, you may be sure that you are moving in the correct direction.

How Is It That They Are Able To Tolerate Confines And Restrictions?

When your kid reaches the point where they feel inwardly linked as a result of you fixing your communication with them (which was discussed in Levels 3 and 4), they will be ready to satisfy the next set of requirements, which is the need to have free choice and agency. Before there is a link between us, they won't be able to fulfill their more important requirements.

It does not matter how effectively you communicate with your kid or how well your child interacts with their peers; there will always be social obstacles since that is just the way the world works. It is essential that your kid participate in meaningful activities that will strengthen their free will and agency so that they will not be highly affected by the problems that they face, such as friends being displeased with them, arguing, feeling wounded, or even being bullied. This will guarantee that your child will not be intensely impacted by the obstacles that they face. Having free will indicates that I, as a spiritual creature, am endowed with the ability to make decisions. I don't have to put unnecessary stress on myself in order to be happy; I can generate that joy on my own. When your kid is aware that they have the ability to make their own decisions, they won't feel obligated to conform to the preferences of their peers or do what they believe is expected of them. A person who has a sense of agency believes that they are worthwhile and helpful, and that they are able to select activities in which they may experience these feelings. When your kid is aware of this, they will be better equipped to handle the few instances in which they find themselves feeling excluded or unnecessary in a social setting. They will be able to take the negative feedback in stride because they will know that yes is more prevalent in their hearts than no.

You are about to acquire the knowledge necessary to strengthen those free will and agency demands that fall into the secondary category.

Little Simon has been acting aggressively toward others, striking and kicking those around him. I've asked him to take a seat for a few minutes so that I can reset, and now he's becoming all huffy about it. I inquire, "Why are you causing harm to other people? What's the matter?" I am aware that young children do not intentionally want to give others harm when they act aggressively against other people, even if they do damage other people. Something within is turned completely on its head. He slowly lets you in on what he's been experiencing. However, the buddy he requested to play with him did not comply with his request. He was quite disappointed. "He doesn't care about me at all! He is not a buddy of mine! That's what Simon told me.

The release of tears is an unavoidable consequence. I despise every single one of them! They are not any of my buddies at all! I'm ready to get out of here!" He cries out in agony, his frail body trembling with anguish. Studies have shown that the neurons in the brain that "light up" in response to physical pain are also activated in response to emotional distress. This suggests that the two types of pain are comparable in their intensity.

I cradle his little body in my arms and murmur soothing words to him. I immediately shift into empathetic mode since now is not the time for me to lecture him about not kicking other people. I give him permission to acknowledge his suffering, "It seems as if you're experiencing a lot of rejection right now. It seems as if you were really looking forward to playing with that buddy, and it seems as though you are experiencing a lot of pain. He calms down and takes his time to reply to me in between whimpers as he settles down.

"I simply can't believe it! He has been quite unkind to me.

I tell them, "You are really getting worked up! What exactly took place?" (I'm practicing H.E.A.R. from Level 3 and trying to identify the behavior that went along with the sensation.)

Together with a handful of his mates, he began excavating mulch to create a mound. It was his buddy who "wouldn't let him use the yellow shovel." As the narrative progresses, I see that Simon didn't want to use any other shovel and instead wanted to steal the yellow shovel from his buddy, who was already using it. This is because the yellow shovel was his favorite shovel. Simon had feelings of rejection and unease as a result of the restrictions that were imposed on him during playtime as a result of the other youngster saying "no." He couldn't stand the sound of the word "no."

The only thing that is expected of me is to put H.E.A.R. into practice. The reprimand for his lack of participation has already been handed out. I don't provide him any other way out of the situation. Now that he's collected himself, he goes off to give it another go. I keep an eye on him throughout the week while he plays and watch him continue to play. Children who are not used to the concept of seeking alternatives when they are told "no" are a source of another degree of social conflict. They give off the impression of being arrogant, self-centered, and excessively dominating.

If your child behaves in this manner, you are most likely shouting at them and telling them, "The world does not revolve around you!" Why aren't you giving anything away? It's not always possible to get what you desire!" This is a red flag that their requirements for free will and agency are not being satisfied.

It's possible that you've noticed that your child gets along best with other kids who are submissive, such as a younger youngster who is willing to listen to their guidance or one that follows them about. It's also possible that they have a lot of older buddies who think they're adorable enough to do anything they want to do. It's possible that this child's interactions as an adult will be marked by an unhealthy power disparity.

One of the most important aspects of leadership is the ability to make choices in a timely and efficient way. The choices you make will have an effect on people's perception of you as a leader as well as the level of confidence they have in you.

Every day, as the battalion head of the fire department, I am tasked with making a wide variety of judgments. I am responsible for making adjustments to the personnel roster before each shift to account for absences caused by vacations, sickness, injuries, or special-duty assignments. In most cases, I have more time on my side when I make judgments like these since they are made in the constraints of an office. On the other side of the spectrum are the choices that I have to make in my role as an incident commander. A fire in a structure will consume both its contents and the building itself at a rate of one doubling in size every seventeen seconds until the firemen are able to halt the progression of the flames. A wildfire that is being pushed by the wind and is burning upward in dry grass, brush, and wood is making quick progress over the landscape. In either circumstance, time is not on my side, and the blazes will not wait for me to come to a conclusion before continuing their spread.

It was a cloudy and chilly day in October of 2006 when I first became interested in the study of how decisions are made. That day, Captain Mike Cerovski, who was the department training officer, and I performed training evolutions for my shift using a contraption that was referred to as the "Christmas tree." The so-called "tree" is really just a vertical pipe that's around 10 feet tall. The look of a tree is achieved by attaching many horizontal pipe branches with tiny holes to the vertical component, which creates the impression of a tree. The appliance is connected to a large propane tank that holds one thousand gallons, and remote control valves are used to regulate the flow of gas. Once the crew has arrived at the location of the fire, the leader of the hose team will be responsible for turning off a valve that is located at the base of the tree.

An evaluation of the company officer's capacity to "size up" (analyze) the situation and devise an initial incident action plan (IAP) is one of the primary goals of an exercise that involves fire as one of its simulated hazards. The IAP is determined by the officer's observations of the situation, the actions that are being taken, and the resources that are required. The goal of fighting any fire is to detect the blaze, contain it, bring it under control, and put it out completely. hunt and rescue, ventilation (the process of creating an opening through which heat and smoke may escape), property protection, and overhaul (the hunt for concealed fire) are additional tasks. In other words, the officer of the corporation is entrusted with making rapid judgments in an atmosphere that is both stressful and chaotic. Because the site of the fire was easily identifiable during this specific exercise, there was no need for search and rescue, ventilation, salvage, or overhaul. Despite this, it was required to carry out all of the other components of the size-up and the IAP.

The officer in training carefully opened the valve to the Christmas tree, and soon after, white propane vapor started to seep out of the holes. I approached the device while outfitted with the necessary personal protection equipment and a self-contained breathing apparatus, also known as a SCBA. I was holding a lighted torch that was hooked by a hose to a twenty-pound cylinder of propane as I walked in the direction of the hissing sound that was being made by propane escaping. Due to the fact that propane is denser than air, I moved the torch in a back-and-forth motion along the ground in order to light the vapor cloud. The pressure of the gas that was escaping was raised by Captain Cerovski, which caused the fire to scream to life, sounding like a little jet engine.

During this time, the three fire departments who were going to participate in the exercise waited at the entrance to our training site. I took the microphone on the radio and keyed it in order to send the companies to 710 South Railroad Avenue, where there was reportedly a propane tank fire that was threatening buildings. Mike opened the gas valve all the way, which caused the flames to become more intense.

In less than a minute, the first engine company arrived, and the lieutenant gave a quick size-up over the radio, explaining what he saw, what he was doing, and what he required. He also said what they needed. There was a hose that was placed out on the ground that was extended out from the engine, but there was no water in the hose. It seemed as if time had stopped moving while the people on board the first engine were having a conversation. I had a hunch that they were deliberating on what action to take next. I sent out a request for assistance from the second engine, and Mike and I both expected that the officer on that rig would assume charge of the issue once it was there. The two teams continued to talk, but nothing further transpired between them. I radioed for the third engine to react, and I was completely prepared for action on their end. The crew exited the engine, made their way to the other two crews, and then joined in on the conversation that was going on. Mike turned to Rick and stated, "Rick, I need to lower the pressure because we're wasting propane."

That's when I made up my mind to take some kind of action. I went up to the gathering and urged them that someone needed to take charge and put an end to the situation as soon as possible. Now! The water began to flow through the hoses, and a lieutenant assumed command of the workers. It was under the protection of a fog stream, which is a wide-angle water stream that resembles a curtain, that he organized two teams of firemen, and they

worked together to drive the fire back until it was possible to access the valve at the foot of the Christmas tree. After the lieutenant reached down and shut off the gas, the blaze was put out, and the crew retreated to where they had been before.

After the exercise was over, we all huddled together and went through what's known as an after-action review, or AAR. The identification of both strong points and problematic areas is one of the goals of an AAR. Discussion of the incident action plan is followed by a comparison of the events that took place. Both the incident response plan and the real-time event should be evaluated in terms of what went well, what didn't go well, and why. And last, what steps need to be taken in order to maintain the progress made in the strong areas and/or make progress in the areas that require improvement?

Attacks against a person's person are not allowed, however each person is required to take responsibility for their actions. Our after-action report shed light on the reason the first arriving officer was not given charge of the situation. Because the fire chief had said that he did not want the first officer to take leadership of an event, he was only following the new direction that had been set by the fire chief. Due to the lack of clarity on what was really going place, the second arriving officer did not assume leadership of the situation. Even the third officer to arrive did not take leadership of the situation. He reasoned that the second officer had assumed leadership based on the directive given by the fire chief, and this was the assumption he made.

Uncertainty, confusion, and disorder were shown among the crews as a result of the AAR. Everyone was at their wit's end. Because no one had assumed authority, there was no risk of the chain of command becoming disorganized.

Why? Because the direction that the fire chief gave to the department broke with time-honored, standard procedures that are followed both locally and nationally. The lack of leadership resulted in a loss of decisiveness, the triumph of hesitation, and the cessation of all activity.

Everyone who participated in the practice was aware of what needed to be done. Every single one of them was a seasoned fireman who was excellent at their professions. There was no issue of ineptitude or a lack of comprehension on this matter. In addition, I have never had any reason to question their expertise, capabilities, or understanding. Because there was no one to make decisions throughout the exercise, it did not go very well. Despite this, the training exercise was ultimately fruitful for everyone involved since they were able to improve their skills as a result of the challenges they faced.

As soon as I took control of the shift, I made it a point to urge everyone to think creatively and outside the box. I assumed that everyone was aware of the meaning of the term since the exact same phrases were used in the after-exercise analysis and reflection. That day, one of the things I learnt was to never assume that other people comprehend what I'm trying to convey to them.

As a battalion leader, one of my responsibilities is to instruct and mentor others, so I said to my subordinates, "Hey, you guys, you need to think outside the box!" I was standing in a small throng that had collected around the rear of a shining red fire engine when all of a sudden I heard a captain question, "What in the world do you mean by thinking outside the box? You repeat this point over and over again, but I have no idea what you're talking about. I was taken aback. Since I took over the shift more than two years ago, he had never once inquired as to what I meant until that afternoon.

His inquiry shed light on a two-pronged issue that needed to be addressed. The first mistake I made was assuming that other people had grasped what I was trying to convey. It doesn't matter how often we or society uses a certain term; not everyone is familiar with it, and not everyone will even bother to find out what it means for themselves. The second issue was that the captain did not inquire about the meaning of the word until after we had participated in an unsatisfactory practice. Aha! The teachable moments throughout one's life.

This is when the irony comes in. At the height of solar storm activity, there is widespread concern that there may be disruptions to communication networks all around the world. However, we do not place the same weight on the interruptions that occur in our regular face-to-face interactions. Miscommunication and misunderstanding have an effect on decision-making, and the repercussions of these two factors may often be rather severe. In the next section of the chapter, I will discuss the repercussions of making decisions.

We are gregarious beings, despite the fact that we are not wolves. People have a strong need to feel connected to one another and included in something larger than themselves. When there are two or more people coming together to create a group, it is inevitable that members of the group will stratify into various roles. Even among the closest of friends, there are always some who prefer to dispute, argue, support, and just hang out with others. There are also those who enjoy to simply be around others. It is possible that friends did not lay the groundwork for the establishment of a vast company; but, the same essential principles of stratification continue to hold true: the corporate board (the "idea" friends), the executive staff, the support staff, and the "ground floor" workers.

Being charismatic and charming are important qualities for leaders, yet such qualities aren't enough. It is not sufficient qualifications for leadership to be gregarious and to have close relationships with other people. To establish a cult of personality around yourself, all you need to do is be accessible and likeable. Unfortunately, this creates difficulties since individuals are unable to be predicted and are subject to change. A leader who is unable to keep up with these changes or who does not stay faithful to their values will, in the end, fail.

According to Types of Leadership Styles and Maryville Online's 2020 research, there are two basic sorts of leaders in general: transformative leadership and transactional leadership. Transactional leadership, which involves a "trade" between the leader and their followers, is the most basic kind of leadership. This transaction is often finalized with the issuance of a paycheck. According to this theory, members of a team make a pact to carry out their leader's orders and finish the task "as given." This outlines everyone's responsibilities and establishes clear standards for each individual member of the team. Due to the fact that success in this model is determined by one's level of performance, it is often successful for those who are competitive and internally motivated by external incentives, such as money, accolades, or possibly a diploma. The disadvantage of this is that it often results in poor morale among those who follow the leader as well as a high turnover rate. This kind of leadership doesn't allow for much of an improvement in staff performance, which stifles innovation and discourages personal growth.

The concept of transformational leadership is becoming more popular in businesses and other types of organizations. According to Types of Leadership Styles and Maryville Online's 2020 article, "Transformational Leadership," the fundamental characteristic of a transformational leader is an ongoing pursuit of innovation and progression. A transformational leader will, in a manner similar to that of a transactional leader, assign duties and responsibilities. But a transformational leader strives to push their followers beyond the boundaries of what is expected of them, despite the fact that everyone has a part to play in the process. They inspire others by encouraging both professional and personal growth in the people who follow them. In essence, transformational leaders serve as a model for others to follow in order to better themselves and their communities. They come up with a set of principles to guide the behavior of their organization, and everyone follows them. They establish unambiguous ethical standards and make it a priority to respect those standards in a consistent manner. They establish a culture that encourages their followers and other people to put the health and happiness of others ahead of their own personal goals and objectives. Followers of the transformational model are educated and guided on how to make choices and take responsibility of their actions via the use of the model.

In 1939, the psychologist Kurt Lewin and his colleagues set out to discover more leadership philosophies (Cherry, 2020). Previously, they had only focused on transactional and transformational leadership styles. Lewin conducted this research with kids and separated them into three groups, each of which was led by a different kind of leader. After that, the researchers led the youngsters in each group through an arts and crafts session while observing their behavior. As a result of this study, Lewin was able to determine that there are three distinct philosophies of leadership: democratic, authoritarian, and laissez-faire. The study conducted by Lewin set the framework for later leadership studies and served as a springboard for the development of more intricate leadership theories.

INTENTION OR AIM

Mark Twain, an American comedian and author, is credited with the famous remark, "The two most important days in your life are the day you're born, and the day you find out why." Today's businesses are required to do in-depth analyses to determine if their goods or services really enrich and improve the lives of the people whose lives they touch. These analyses must also take into account other externalities, such as the influence their operations have on the environment and the society in which they operate. This begins with top executives being involved in a conversation about the "why": Why do we exist, and why do we attempt to provide beyond merely competing customer needs and profits? How does the recruitment strategy of an organization evolve so that it can serve its purpose? During the recruiting process, there is a big chance lost to determine an applicant's level of conviction and enthusiasm for the organization's overall mission. Many executives will, by nature, be inquisitive and search for ways to tie the mission of the firm to their own personal goals.

The following aspects of organizational purpose will be discussed in this chapter: What exactly is it? To what end does it serve? How do you explain the objective of the position to candidates? How exactly do you define culture, purpose, and engagement in the recruitment process, and how do you go about creating alignment? How exactly do you assist customers and applicants in locating one another having a certain goal in mind?

To start, however, let's talk about what we mean when we say "purpose." The purpose of a firm, as opposed to a normal mission statement, seeks to answer the question of why the organization operates in the manner in which it does. In addition to outlining the broad course the company will take, it may also include specifics such as main emphasis areas, strategic relationships, and target consumers. One further explanation that differentiates mission, vision, and purpose may be that a solid mission statement and vision statement are best suited for providing internal organizational direction. This would be an example of a definition that explains the distinction between mission, vision, and purpose. Purpose, on the other hand, helps you to maintain a focus on the reason for your being. Your purpose will enable you to choose how you will go about achieving your vision, which will connect you with your aim. A supporter will have faith in your organization's mission when they feel a connection to your cause. A meaningful and permanent reason for an organization to exist, its mission provides an answer to the question "why." What are we doing this for? Why are we engaging in commercial activity? It is the primary purpose for the existence of the organization. The organizational purpose should be aligned with the long-term financial performance, should offer a clear framework for everyday decision-making, should unify and motivate key stakeholders, and should be communicated to all relevant stakeholders. The most crucial thing that has to be done for the company in order for it to achieve sustainable development is to realign itself with its goal. If people are working hard with the best of intentions, but they are not aligned with the purpose of the firm, then their productivity may be at odds with the objectives that are necessary for the company's long-term success.

To instill a sense of purpose into a whole organization, one must begin at the very top. When workers see their leaders connected to a mission, they will feel more connected to that purpose themselves. Only executives and workers who are emotionally invested in the mission of a firm will be able to steer it toward the achievement of its objectives. When workers buy into the mission of their employer, it will pave the way for increased creativity, collaboration, and overall organizational success. Companies that have well defined goals and values will often and openly discuss their goals and values. They talk about it in commercials and at all levels of the company, as well as publish it on their websites and in printed materials, hang it up on the walls of the workplace, and show it there. According to statistics, only approximately 70 percent of the workforce is interested in the job that they do, and the leading cause of disengagement is inadequate leadership. Because of this, having leaders who are linked to the company's mission will result in employees who are engaged in their job and who are also committed to the company's purpose.

Ideology is not the same thing as purpose. As was said before, this approach is one that is focused on the bottom line and offers an edge to competitors. Not only a salary, but meaningful employment is becoming more important to today's workforce. As an example, if a construction worker is requested to dismantle a playground for children, it is quite probable that the motivation behind the request is not only based on the potential money from doing so. At the end of the day, they would most likely be curious to learn the reason why. After that, are they going to construct one that is either superior or more aesthetically pleasing? Or is it just to create room for a brand new petrol station that is being built? Knowing makes a significant impact. If recruiters are able to explain the purpose of the business to potential candidates, they will be in a better position to choose leaders who are driven by the same objectives and are more likely to make a significant contribution to the company in a shorter amount of time.

Finding individuals that are driven by the same goal as the organization and who are inspired by the mission of the organization can help you establish teams that believe in the purpose of your firm as well. To emphasize this point, in our own experience in making offers to a large number of very senior executive candidates, we would cover in our conversation all of the standard salary and benefits items that were a part of the offer as normal and pretty rapidly. These items included a range of options, including health insurance, retirement plans, and paid time off. However, the page in the discussion paper that the candidates appeared to linger on the most and want to speak more about was the one that highlighted the influence that they were going to have on the product, the company, and the industry. Out of all the components of the offer, they were most interested in the "why." If you have ever questioned why a candidate would accept a career that paid less than what they were earning at their existing job, you now know the answer to that question: The reason.

Your responsibility as a recruiter is to explain to prospects what the company does and why it exists. Employees cannot be required to comply with this requirement in any way. The process of recruiting new employees provides a chance for both parties to discover a natural alignment between the goals of the person and those of the business. Recruiters also have a huge chance here to evaluate the prospects' level of conviction and enthusiasm from the very beginning of the process. One of the most important methods that every recruiter has to put into practice throughout the recruiting process is giving top priority to communication that is both succinct and clear. Check to see that there is no space for misunderstanding the situation. When it is clearly stated, the mission of an organization is always straightforward and simple to grasp. Providing instances of how it is viewed in the company is one of the things that helps improve its worth.

Taking Steps Towards The Creation

The encouraging thing is that one may be taught to perceive things from an opportunity-based perspective. It is not a consistent aspect of one's character. It is a talent that can be honed with dedication and consistent practice. One of the most exciting achievements in recent years in the fields of neuroscience and positive psychology has been the discovery that personality characteristics and even the brain itself are malleable. These breakthroughs are essential to leadership as well as coaching in general. And I couldn't have gotten by without them.

My previous pattern of seeing every new event as either terrible luck or good fortune, with the emphasis being on the former, was called into question by my coach, which is one of the numerous advantages I have personally experienced as a result of receiving coaching. He would listen to my most recent dilemma with patience and compassion, and he would hear the victimized context I was placing it in until I finally got it off my chest. At that moment, he would welcome me into the realm of possibility, which appeared to be the place from whence he always emerged.

He would often inquire, "Are you willing to open up a little bit and play with this?"

Naturally, I was one of them. I was investing a lot of money in the coaching, so I knew I couldn't avoid facing the issues head-on during our sessions, despite the fact that I first found them to be rather painful.

He asked me whether I was willing to see beyond the issue and recognize the treasure that was hidden inside it. He would make statements such as, "What's nice about this? The question is, "Where is the opportunity?" And after a long and creative brainstorming session with them, I would start to see things that I had been blind to while I was stuck in my tiny self, my victim self, and clinging closely to the narrative of misfortune that I had concocted on my own.

Consolidating The Roots Of Your Educational Tree

When we are trying to learn anything new, one of the most common errors that we make is that we do not spend enough time and effort on the basics. Continuing with the metaphor of a tree, it adds several branches and a large number of leaves to our tree without making any effort to reinforce the trunk. Now, you may be wondering: why is this such a significant issue?

It is an issue because it causes us to overload our system with an excessive amount of information that is unnecessary and unimportant, as well as knowledge that is just too much for us to process all at once.

As a direct consequence of this, we won't be able to remember very much of what we study. People sometimes lament that they have a terrible memory, and although it is undeniably true that everyone's memories are unique, it is also true that people's memories may vary greatly. Encoding problems, on the other hand, are more likely to be the source of headaches than memory problems. That is to say, since they haven't constructed a firm basis for their learning (a sturdy tree trunk), they don't have anything to which they can connect all of the new knowledge that they're striving to absorb.

I'll illustrate this point using a real-world scenario. You put in the time to read a three hundred page book on how to improve your learning. While you are doing so, a lot of information, including the following items, is probably coming at you nonstop:

Anecdotes only tangentially connected to the themes explored in the book

dozens of suggestions or pieces of advise

Learning, as investigated by scientific inquiry

Various accounts

Statistics, as well as

Words or ideas that are foreign to you.

The majority of the aforementioned objects may be thought of as branches or leaves attached to the trunk of the tree. If you let yourself to get too distracted by them and assign them more value than the trunk (important ideas, major themes, and so on), you will experience feelings of being overwhelmed and will remember very little from the book.

And yet, this is something that we often do. We are unable to differentiate between crucial bits of information and other pieces of information that are less significant. It is important to keep in mind that not all knowledge is created equal, as I indicated before when I was discussing learning myths. You shouldn't worry about adding extra branches, leaves, or ornaments to your tree; instead, you should concentrate on making it stronger. If you don't keep it up, it will fall apart, which means you won't remember much of what you've been "learning."

As a result, one of the most important things to consider at all times is, "what's the trunk here?"

Where is the meat of this discussion located?

Where does the story really go in this chapter?

Where is the hidden treasure in this book?

Where is the storage compartment in this video?

For example, what's the main focus of this part of the article? What is the most important point you have to take away from this?

The crucial point is that, when you're trying to learn anything new, you should concentrate on finding the most important ideas and facts and becoming an expert on them.

You will be able to have a strong foundation upon which to develop additional knowledge if you carry out the steps outlined in the sentence.

Let's take a more in-depth look at the meaning behind the "tree trunk" symbol that appears in the overall structure of this book.

Response and Forwarding

When you are in a leadership position, it is essential to provide feedback. Just keep in mind one thing for now. Always focus on the actions rather than the person you are discussing. Your comments need to focus on particulars rather than being too generic. When providing comments, try to steer clear of utilizing the term "you." Be sure that the person receiving the criticism has the ability to change the aspect of their performance that is being criticized. Instead of stating, "You are always late," try saying something like this. You may begin by saying something along the lines of, "Lars, I wanted to chat to you today regarding attendance. Is there anything that you think I need to be aware of that's happening right now?" It is likely that you will find out that they were late three times over the previous week due to a domestic issue or an accident. This is a possibility. Certain individuals are hesitant to discuss personal concerns with figures of authority, particularly if the authority figures are relatively new. It's really crucial to get feedback. at the past, I worked at a manufacturing facility. One day, my boss was on the other side of the factory, and we were aware that he expected all of our equipment to be operational when he returned. That day, he did not reveal which guy would be in charge of which function. We all headed to a station, where we started operating various sections. When he came around again, he motioned for me to come over to the side of the room and questioned why I wasn't using a certain equipment. It was the one that had the largest components being made on it, therefore it was presumably the one that required most precision. He questioned me, "Why aren't you running machine number 1? You are the best at running that one, and your quality is good. Why aren't you running machine number 1?" I have more faith in you than in anybody else about it." Do you know the response I gave you? "Because you never told me that I was good at it." I informed him about it. You need to understand that despite being an effective manager, he was not the kind of person who offered constructive criticism. He never informed me that he intended me to operate those components and that equipment in the past; rather, he just assumed that I was aware of his expectations. You might also attempt making use of a method that's known as feedforward. Feedforward is quite similar to feedback, with the key difference being that it does not concentrate on the past. It will happen at a later time. Additionally, it is often the recipient who makes the first move. The question "What can I do to ensure that you complete your assigned tasks every day?" is an example of this kind of inquiry. Request that people be honest in their replies, and refrain from passing judgment on the individual you are questioning. Simply express gratitude to the individual for their contribution, and then proceed. When you use feedforward, you may often get some very helpful information. Check out this book if you want to learn more about feedforward. A book written by Marshall Goldsmith titled "What Got You Here Won't Get You There."

In the event that you sound the alarm in the middle of an emergency, nobody will want to be near to you since you are the leader.In point of fact, everyone need to keep their distance from you!

A state of emergency is not the time to lose your composure and panic. Now is the moment to maintain your composure! When you converse while in a state of stress, you end up conveying your panic to the other person.

The irony of competence:

A great number of people who are competent in terms of their talents, gifts, and experience are unable to progress in life because they need assurance. Remember that having the capacity is important, but having the confidence to use it is critical. Whenever two people work along amicably, the one who has the greater amount of conspicuous assurance has the benefit. It should come as no surprise that the word "advantage" originates from the archaic sport of arm wrestling. The one who comes out on top gets his hand placed on top of the hand of the loser. He is in a better position. Simply said, if you want to come out on top in your administration sport, you need to have a higher level of confidence.

CONFIDENCE IS RELATED TO AN INCREASE IN THE FOLLOWING SEVEN QUALITIES:

1. Having courage

2. an attitude of mental composure

3. The ability to think clearly

4. Independence from external direction

5. Capacity to overcome hardship when it arises

6. a certain mind-set

7. Quickness of response

If you go back through history, you'll find that the great majority of the outstanding pioneers whose contributions we value now didn't start out with all of the essential capabilities. Despite this, they participated in a variety of causes because they thought it was necessary. They felt more confident in their decisions the further they got engaged. The more confident they were, the more adept they became at what they were doing. The ability to patiently wait for something beautiful may prove to be ageless. Start out with the conviction that you will eventually acquire the talent.

CONFIDENCE In Contrast With ARrogance

People often inquire as to the differences between absolute confidence and pompous behavior. The characteristics of unjustified childishness and disinterest for the viewpoints and significance of other people are characteristics of arrogance. The principle is as follows: The notion that I am capable of doing anything at all is arrogance. The belief that I am capable of doing this task is the essence of certainty.

A SCRIPT TO KICK-START YOUR CONFIDENCE

The ever-evolving recognition of one's own capabilities is the foundation of confidence. Your past experiences, worries, and frailties may have an effect on your assurance; nonetheless, you shouldn't let this deter you from moving forward. A powerless mental self image is the starting point for an absence of assurance. Find strategies to bolster the mental image of yourself that you have of yourself, and you will start to acquire a sense of assurance. People are drawn to those that exude confidence via the way they carry themselves, communicate, and interact with others.

Make a note of the things that are true about you, the things that are unique about you, and the wonderful things that others have said about you. Write them all down. It is not necessary for there to be a significant amount or importance. Nevertheless, it has to be authentic, positive, and distinct. Read through the Confidence launch script on a regular basis as well as any number of times you see necessary in order to assist yourself in remembering your positive qualities and accomplishments. It's possible that you're not giving proper credit to your successes and the good things that have happened to you, but that's not always the case. When good things start to occur in your life, be sure to include them into your writing as soon as possible. The development of your content will parallel the growth of your conviction. This will progressively strengthen your mental self-view and transform you from someone who is skillful into someone who is equipped and assured of themselves. Your behavior begins to shift in accordance with the beliefs that you have. Reading my self-assurance script, recording it on my phone, and listening to it a few times in the morning or whenever I feel like I need an extra boost is a technique that I've found to be beneficial. I also find that recording it and listening to it when I'm feeling particularly down is effective.

What does this have to do with anything? In the event that you do not have trust in yourself, no one else will. Self-assurance is a skill, and just like any other competence, you may develop it more through time.

Check out the Mousetrap Resource Center if you are in need of serious help in creating the launch script for your Confidence application.

Conventions Governing Businesses Often Require Participation In Negotiations

During the time that I was attending school at an engineering school, I was witness to an event that was very fascinating. One of my male friends wanted me to set up a conversation between him and one of my female friends so that he could apologize to her for something that he had previously said to her. Despite the lack of clarity in my comprehension of the situation, I was willing to concede. At the cafeteria of our academic institution, I paid a visit to a female friend without first letting her know that I was accompanied by a male buddy. I convinced myself that I was engaged in the honorable work of minimizing the disparities that existed between two individuals (both of whom were my friends). When my buddy's girlfriend came in, we were having a cup of tea in the canteen together. I was there with my male friend. To my astonishment, she immediately began shouting aggressively at my male companion! I was taken aback when she reprimanded me and said that her faith in me had diminished as a result of that particular occurrence. She departed. After some time had passed, I found out that my male buddy had severely insulted her at an earlier point in time. I greatly regret the fact that I played the "go-between" position between the two parties without consulting my female friend first, and I apologized to her for doing so. In addition, I admonished my male buddy for keeping the specific purpose of the meeting a secret from me in the context of the situation.

An error in communication was made when I failed to inform my female buddy about my male friend and the context of the situation when we were meeting; in other words, the communication did not go in both directions.

From a psychological point of view: Communication refers to an encounter that is meaningful and is based on feedback. It is impossible to say that communication has taken place between two or more parties unless there has been a "exchange and acceptance" of the respective offers or declarations. The cognitive architecture of humans demonstrates that communications have been going around in order to clarify the inter-personal understanding, the understanding between person and organization, or the understanding between organization and organization. A definitive proclamation of the communication pretext should be made prior to the realization of the scheduled convention. When the conscious mind and the subconscious mind (the part of the mind that stores memories from the past) are not in sync with one another, conflict occurs, and the communication goal becomes hazy. And if this kind of misunderstanding is realized, then it will lead to disputes and confrontations, which will ultimately result in losses for companies.

BUSINESS LESSON: Whenever we organize a meeting for the purpose of negotiating or establishing consensus, the contextual backdrop should be very apparent among all of the individuals participating in the discussion; otherwise, the interaction goal at the meeting will end out poorly.

Harmonizing the Pace and Tone

However, in truth, a significant lot of information is represented via our tone, much more so than the words that we choose to communicate with. This is one reason why tone of voice is so seldom employed to its full potential.

The speaker's rapid speed and loud tone are telltale signs that they are stressed, worried, or even afraid.

A monotonous tone and a plodding pace are signs of either boredom or melancholy.

Excitation and/or fury might be inferred from a tone and speed that are both rapid and irregular.

Insecurities are communicated with a low loudness and tone.

The speed and tone of the music should be light and rhythmic to convey enjoyment.

A confident and competent demeanor is communicated with an even tempo and an appropriately varied tone.

When having a conversation with someone, pay close attention to the tone of their voice and make an effort to determine the underlying state of mind that they are in at the moment. After getting a notion of how they are feeling, pick an emotional state that you want them to be in. The next step is to quietly mimic their tone and tempo as precisely as possible, and after that, gradually alter both your tone and pace in order to guide them into a new positive mood.

Practice each of the aforementioned strategies and procedures in isolation, one at a time, until you have mastered them all and they come naturally to you. You won't be able to use these abilities naturally at first, but with enough practice, you'll be able to internalize them and use them in any manner that's appropriate for the circumstance, whether you use them alone or in combination.

156